Winning the B2B Sale in China

By c.j. Ng

Copyright © 2021

All rights reserved.

ISBN: 9798499847978

Winning the B2B Sale in China

CONTENTS

1	The Evolution of Relationship Selling in China	5
2	The Myths and Truths about Building Strong Relationships with Customers	19
3	How to Sell to Customers When They Don't Have an Obvious Need?	39
4	Managing Your Relationships With Key Stakeholders	54
5	Relationship Pricing	70
6	Engaging With Internal Stakeholders to Fulfill External Customers' Needs	85
7	Motivating and Developing Your Sales Team	98

Winning the B2B Sale in China

Prelude

My name is c.j.. I'm a Chinese Singaporean. I came to Shanghai, China, in 2004. I then spent the next 16 years working with several sales organizations across China, including regional sales offices, individual sales teams, and distributor networks of various industries, company sizes, and ownership backgrounds. .

In 2005 I joined an industrial media company called Ringier Trade Publishing as Sales Training Manager for the Greater China region, where I was responsible for developing the capabilities of our sales teams. In addition to conducting sales training workshops for our sales people, I often accompanied them during sales calls to observe them in action. At the same time, I met with our customers, which included their General Managers and Sales Directors. The industries I covered ranged from plastics molding to machine tooling and industrial automation.

I am also a witness to how sales methods evolved in China. In 2007 I began my journey of becoming a facilitator, coach, and consultant. I worked with more companies in a broader range of industries, including IT, hospitality, and medical devices, among others. I've had the honor of deep conversations with different levels of people in my clients' organizations, from sales reps to their managers, right up to their top management. I've collected numerous stories based on these insights, and it's my pleasure to share some of these stories in this book.

China's evolution in the field of business-to-business selling is still ongoing, and I will continue be an active participant in this evolution. The following pages serve as a summary of this evolution up to this point, as well as a starting point for your business adventures in China. Look for more exciting exploits waiting to be written in the not-too-distant future!

Part 1

The Evolution of Relationship Selling in China

Winning the B2B Sale in China

While China is rapidly changing in terms of its economy, society, and technology, its nature remains relationships or guanxi-focused. Here's a real-life case unfolding when I first wrote about it, which will change whatever perceptions you had about guanxi and how to deal with it.

Years ago, I met a friend who specialized in cultivating good guanxi with government officials in small towns across China. The objective was to explore any infrastructural projects in that town and then leverage the guanxi or relationship with the local official to get the deal.

It didn't matter if my friend had the right expertise or experience handling such projects for a long time. As long as the official nods his head (yes, in almost every case, they are male), my friend gets the deal. Of course, parts of the proceeds from such arrangements will be "donated" to these officials.

Before clinching such deals, my friend would go about his fair share of dining and entertaining these officials to cultivate the guanxi. Such "bonding" activities include:

- Paying for the officials (and his family sometimes) for "business trips" to Shanghai (the business of shopping and eating, that is),
- Paying for the officials and their buddies for their day/ night outs at the golf courses, KTVs, and other adult entertainment venues,
- Providing gifts to the official's family

members, which sometimes can be paying for the officials' children to attend overseas universities or other offerings..

Needless to say, as China later began cracking down hard on corruption, my friend found it harder and harder to do business with these officials. However, the turning point came in a fascinating twist.

As usual, my friend had cultivated very good guanxi with the mayor of a small town, which happened to need some new street lamps. Having invested years of hard work (and hard-earned funds) in cultivating the guanxi, my friend was very confident he would get the deal.

One fine day though, he got a call from another person who claimed to be his competitor to bid for the street lamps. The competitor told my friend he knew about all that was happening between my friend and the mayor, AND that this competitor had the expertise as well as the right hardware to be the much better solution. The competitor then offered my friend a "withdrawal fee" of RMB 500,000. If my friend withdrew from the project, he would be paid RMB 500,000 (which was a lot of money back then, but probably petty cash these days!).

Having complete confidence in his guanxi with the mayor, and not believing this competitor had the connections to win the project, my friend chose to go ahead with the bidding.

Sure enough, during the day of the bidding, the

competitor turned up with all the product samples, blueprints, and supporting documents to show they were the professionals in this business. My friend only presented a few pieces of paper that didn't say much. The mayor had to award a small part of the business to the competitor. In a bid to salvage the situation, offered my friend to return with the missing product samples and detailed specifications on a future date to bid for the more significant part of the business.

That was NOT the end yet. As my friend didn't have the required expertise in this field, he had to borrow more money to fund the product samples, as well as hire some lighting engineers to provide detailed specifications. All this with no guarantee that after having done all this, he would actually get the business.

At this point, you might think the mayor was not trustworthy, and the years of guanxi cultivation were not delivering any results. The truth, however, might be more complex than that.

The biggest question was how the competitor knew about the dealings between my friend and the mayor, besides getting the information about project scope. Wasn't the mayor the key decision maker in this deal? If so, why and how could such a turn of events happen?

While we would never know exactly how the competitor got all this information, we certainly could make educated guesses of what might have happened.

One of the fundamental mistakes my friend and many salespeople made was to assume the key decision-maker had all the support of his colleagues. While most subordinates show reverence to their superiors, that might NOT necessarily mean they truly respect and obey their leaders. Some of them might have a hidden agenda to make their bosses trip and fall, so they could step and be the successors.

As a result, even though you might have an edge with strong guanxi, it does not automatically mean you are sure to get the deal.

While cultivating the right relationships is still a very important aspect of doing business and getting deals in China today, the nature of such relationships was fast-changing. It changed from "what I can personally gain by giving the deal to you", to "how can you help me do a better job so I can look great in front of my superiors".

When cultivating or nurturing relationships with Chinese customers, here's what salespeople will now have to be mindful of:

- Could there be silent opposition in the customer's organization that could jeopardize your deal? If yes, what could you do about it?
- What would be a safe, ethical and rewarding way to cultivate a trusting relationship?

Winning the B2B Sale in China

Pivot to Building Trusting Relationships

While the sales training universe focuses on consultative style selling, the relationship part has been overlooked, as if it was terrible or irrelevant. That could be a mistake in many Asian countries, particularly in China.

When salespeople sell products or solutions that may be very complex or challenging for the customer to understand, customers might want to clarify those issues from trusted sources. These trusted sources could be where they can find unbiased information or ask people with whom they have a trusting relationship. As such, developing trusting relationships is an integral part of selling, and sales organizations ignore this fact at their peril.

As sales organizations transition from selling boxes to selling integrated solutions, salespeople will have to adjust the ways they sell. In addition, as customers transition from buying boxes to buying integrated solutions, the contact people involved might have changed, and their expectations of how the salesperson handles the sales conversation may have changed. Instead of having the sales conversation around products, salespeople will have to strike up conversations with customers revolving around business and technical issues that could benefit the customer in some ways. Thus, the key challenge for sales organizations is to implement ways to change the mindsets of salespeople who are used to selling or peddling products, then equip them with the skills to strike up engaging conversations with the customer.

At the same time, though, there are also many misconceptions about relationship selling. While selling in China has evolved a lot over the last 20 years, salespeople will need to be aware of particular quirks in this market. Some salespeople are selling in this market as if they were selling 20 years ago in China.

6 Common Sales Mistakes When Selling in China

1. Guanxi Misconceptions

- When someone mentions "guanxi", what springs to mind is entertaining customers at the KTV and providing certain "services" to clients that may not be compliant.
- What most salespeople don't understand is that at the core of any relationship is trust. As such, the entire premise of relationship building is about increasing mutual trust between buyer and seller..
- Customers make buying decisions because they care, which brings an emotional aspect to every buying decision. Today's salespeople need to learn how to connect emotionally with the customer through the trust they have established with the customer..

2. Chasing Leads That Lead Nowhere

- Generally, salespeople are excited when

customers make contact for a sales inquiry. Sometimes this takes the form of a prospective customer whom the salespeople have been trying to do business with, contacting the salesperson out of the blue to invite the salesperson for last-minute bidding on a substantial deal.
- I believe many of us have experienced such scenarios in the past, and there are clear signs the invitation was for a second or third bidder. Unfortunately, some salespeople can be pressured to follow every lead, even though such leads lead them nowhere. This could be in the form of being the second or third bidder or chasing after customers who are a poor fit for the seller's products, services, and prices.

3. Price is NOT the No. 1 Factor

- The general perception is the Chinese market is very price-driven, and many salespeople lose their sales due to price reasons. While there certainly are some truths in this verdict, the details are much more complex.
- While price tends to be a key consideration in many purchases, it is hardly the only determining factor. Salespeople are more successful when they can help the customer understand the difference between their price and the actual purchase cost.

4. Aligning with the Buying Process

- Sometimes sales people tend to contact the people they already know, such as the purchasing manager or technical people, rather than the people they need to reach out to as decision makers. These could be the senior management and key buying influencers of the customer's organisations.
- Sales people also tend to enter into the sales process far too late and find themselves unable to influence customers.

5. Not Asking Questions to Gain Insights

- By now many salespeople in China have gone through many sales training programmes, and most of these programmes would have taught salespeople to ask questions.
- However, the purpose of asking questions is to gain insights into how customers think or feel about specific issues. Salespeople interrogate many customers, or the questions raised tend to yield very superficial responses that do not provide any valuable insights.

6. High Costs of Lead Generation

- Many sales people in China rely on trade shows as the primary means of generating leads. While trade shows are good ways to find prospective customers, the cost of participating in trade shows can be prohibitive.

- In a market where customers and competitors are growing exponentially, salespeople in China would have to seek alternative ways to generate more qualified leads to grow their business. Besides building excellent personal rapport with your customers, perhaps you can also take time to understand the customers' overall concerns to provide better and more creative solutions that work.

Relationship Building in a Compliant Environment

Charlie thought he had his client well in hand. He felt he had fully grasped his client's situation. His client, the Purchasing Manager, was in his late-20's, had recently purchased a house, and had a baby, AND his salary was meager. Charlie thought a person in such a situation would need or at least like to have some cash to keep up with family expenses. Charlie knew his client needed more money.

Since Charlie worked for a foreign company in China, he would not bribe his client. However, Charlie had it all planned out. His company supplied products to distributors at a much lower discounted price than end customers' prices if they were to buy directly.

Due to this factor, the distributor had enough margin to fork out from the price differential and bribe the customer. Charlie worked with a couple of "distributors" whose roles were NOT to grow the market for Charlie's employer, BUT whose sole purpose was to "help foreign companies do the things these companies weren't allowed to".

Charlie knew if he were to give his client enough money, this could be the key differentiator in a highly competitive industry. He knew this customer was "in the bag," so to speak. He had the "guanxi".

Unfortunately for Charlie the client eventually bought from someone else and not from Charlie. Thinking the competitor might have given more money than he did, Charlie tried to ask his client if his "offer" was too low.

The client politely told Charlie the competitor did not offer any bribes at all. They won the bid because they paid more attention to the client's company's needs, not his financial situation. The client thanked Charlie for his "thoughtfulness", and told Charlie to keep in touch.

A few months later, a whistleblower exposed Charlie's "under the table" practices, and both Charlie and his distributor were arrested. Charlie's boss was not spared, either. He was fined, and promptly fired from his job for not safeguarding the reputation and integrity of the company.

If you were to ask a corrupt sales person why he bribes his customers, chances are the answers could be:

- Because everybody was doing it,
- Because every customer asked for it, and

- If we don't do it, we will lose the business.

However, some companies have rigorous policies and corporate governance and ensure their staff does not have an opportunity to bribe their customers.

For these companies, it was found that:

- Even if their sales people DON'T bribe their customers, they could still win sales,
- These companies sell to both foreign and Chinese companies, and they are still able to win sales from all kinds of companies WITHOUT bribing, and
- While having no bribes (or even gifts) may make the sales process more challenging, such obstacles can still be overcome and generate sales!

Some explanations could be:

- While some customers may remain corrupt and expect some kind of kick-backs, most of them would put their company's interests BEFORE their personal interests. That is, the acceptance of a bribe must be made ONLY if their boss's/ management's requirements have been met FIRST. Hence, if you can meet your customers' expectations while your corrupt competitors can't, you can still get the sale.
- Some customers with very rigorous anti-corruption practices would only buy from

- those who are just as strict.
- Some buyers may be concerned that if they were to be seen as corrupt and accepting kick-backs, it might hurt their future career advancement and reputation.

In other words, you CAN sell without bribing in China, AND there will always be the risk of getting caught and severely punished.

It was also interesting to observe that:

- If a salesperson began his career in a company where bribing is condoned, that sales person may still have a mindset he cannot sell without bribing, AND
- If a salesperson started his career in a company where bribing and other types of corruption were NOT tolerated, that sales person would look into the different ways of selling without bribing the customer!

There are several areas companies will have to address to make sure their sales people come clean with their sales strategies. When setting the right systems and policies, companies will have to:

- Ensure there are no loopholes that corrupt sales people, distributors or customers can capitalize on, and
- Review existing sales and sales channel policies to make sure the system is not being exploited.

Sales people need to be briefed, trained or even

indoctrinated on the do's and don'ts of doing business. They also need to understand WHY they had to adhere to strict regulations.

Finally, it's not simply enough to enforce company policies. Sales people need to be equipped with the skills to handle some customers' kick-back requests, hopefully with the possibility of closing the sale remaining intact.

Senior management needs to be willing to walk away and not deal with unethical customers. Some issues bothering senior managers may include:

- If we were to turn away those unethical customers, could we still meet our growth targets? Would we then lose market share to our competitors? and
- If we were to rein in our top sales people and distributors, would they leave the company, thus crippling it's sales results?

On the one hand, you have to develop trusting relationships to get good sales results in China and much of Asia. On the other hand, you would need to ensure how to do so ethically and comply with legal requirements. The challenge for managers is to look into developing trusting, long-term relationships rather than short-term and non-compliant ones.

Part 2

The Myths and Truths about Building Strong Relationships with Customers

Winning the B2B Sale in China

If you were to look at any form of relationship, be that husband-wife, parent-child, or between friends or colleagues, the basis of ALL relationships is trust. If you have strong mutual trust, you will have stronger relationships. If you have weaker trust, you have more fragile relationships.

In the sales context, when customers trust you more, it is more likely they will buy from you. Considering products or solutions you sell can be rather complex even for technically savvy customers, you will need to ask questions to find out what configurations will address the customer's needs and pains. Presenting your solution to them, so they understand how your solution will work will increase success. Without sufficient trust, customers are not going to open up and share their vulnerabilities with you. If they don't trust you enough, they will be rather suspicious about the solutions you provide and question your reliability as a vendor.

So, the more complex solution you are selling, the more you need to develop trust and relationships with your customers.

When someone mentions anything to do with developing good relationships with customers, images of wining, dining, and other forms of entertainment tend to flash in our heads.

Why do we equate relationship building to wining and dining?

Somehow, this has to do with how we build trust

with others. We can understand this from the following angles:

- People tend to be more open and forthright when they are relaxed. People tend to be more relaxed when they are wining and dining in an informal setting.
- People like others who are like them. If people can find opportunities to share common interests, topics, or shared experiences, this builds trust.
- People like to be with those who bring joyful moments.

Making customers happy by entertaining them is a way of building trust. However, developing customer relationships through wining and dining is a very narrowly defined aspect of relationships. Certain elements may be overlooked, such as:

- Just because you gave a customer a great time does not mean you can take care of the customer's business or technical needs.
- You may not have a large entertainment budget, and you certainly want to be compliant in how you deal with your customers.
- Some customers avoid wining and dining with salespeople anyway.

In other words, customers buy from people they trust and respect, and not necessarily with the people they like. That does not mean you make customers dislike you. It just means merely by making your customer like you does not and will not guarantee sales.

So how do you then develop trust and relationships with customers without wining and dining? If you look at how trust works in a work scenario, there are at least two levels of trust:

- Trust in your integrity (that you won't hurt them), and
- Trust in your ability (that you can get things done for them).

While wining and dining with customers allows you to know each other outside of work, it does not help either party assess their ability to get things done or the other party's integrity.

Here are some of the things that build trust with customers you or your company may already be doing:

- Reputable company or brand,
- Experience handling similar industries or situations.
- Sharing technical expertise.
- Product demonstrations.
- Referrals from others.

These actions, while effective, are just scraping the surface of the iceberg. There are more things a salesperson can do to develop trust with a customer. To build deeper trust and relationships with a customer, the salesperson needs to be empathetic with the customer.

The term "tactical empathy" was coined by former FBI negotiator Chris Voss. It is defined as "the process of knowingly and intentionally influencing your counterpart's emotions to make deals…you demonstrate you recognize the other side's perspective and can articulate it in a strategic, even proactive manner — even when you don't like their perspective!"

Case Study: How to Build Trust by Forgoing Short Term Gains for Long Term Profits

One of my sales coachees, John, presented this scenario. The company he's working for imports certain welding products into China. The business was great as the quality and functionality of the imported products were much better than those made in China.

However, over the years, some of those China-made products have improved their quality. They were now comparable with the imported ones but at lower prices. Increasingly, John found it harder to convince customers to buy his company's products with comparable ones in the market at a much more attractive price.

After much discussion, we found that:

- Customers would still like to work with John's company, as some of their products still have a competitive edge over the locally produced ones.
- Customers also appreciated getting the company's technical expertise, which

customers tap into for technical advice and creating technical frameworks.
- John began to generate more sales by winning more bids rather than competing with local suppliers based on price.
- The company was also going through localizing production, which will reduce prices and lead time in the next 1-2 years.

John decided to use some tactical empathy and step into the customer's shoes. He realized that if he could maintain trust with his customers, he would provide his products at more competitive prices with better lead times soon. However, if the trust is eroded, he might lose his customers forever.

So, he began to advise customers proactively:

- What products the customer needs to import, as that is critical to their success,
- What products the customer can choose to procure locally, as those are less critical and the locally-made ones have comparable quality and functions,
- Which local providers have better reputations than others, and which ones the customer should consider if they want to source locally, and most importantly
- How customers can transit or integrate between imported and locally-made equipment so the customer can have a smoother implementation.

In doing so, the salesperson faced a lot of pressure

and backlash from his managers who saw this as sacrificing the company's sales revenues.

However, within months, John found he was invited to bid for more projects by customers and won more bids as a result. Customers were also giving him more referrals, as they knew John would be impartial when giving advice. The new business generated more than compensated for the initial lost sale.

At the same time, John's customers were very keen on buying locally produced products from his company. They liked the products in the first place, but they loved dealing with John, so much so that they would buy from him if his products were priced slightly higher than the competition.

By being empathetic about the customers' longer-term needs, John built more vital trust and stronger relationships with his customers. This led to better sales and profits.

How to Build Trust with Decadent Customers using Tactical Empathy

One of my other sales coachees, Michael, lamented he could not build deeper relationships with one of his customers. While he could gain trust by helping to resolve this customer's business and technical challenges, he simply could not get into the "inner circle" of the customer and foster deeper relationships. As such, he could not discover potential business that could be in the pipeline, or the customer's deeper concerns.

While this customer led a more decadent lifestyle, and frequently visited nightclubs and KTVs along with his suppliers, Michael was a family man and avoided certain forms of customer "entertainment". Besides, Michael's company's compliance policies also forbade their salespeople from bringing customers to nightclubs and KTVs.

Since Michael did not hang out with him in these entertainment venues, the customer felt there seemed to be a lack of common language outside of work.. This led to a mutual feeling of distance between them.

After some coaching, we concluded Michael did not need to be decadent to build rapport with this customer. Michael did not even need to judge the customer based on the latter's lifestyle preferences. All Michael needed to do was to practice tactical empathy and be a good listener. We also knew this customer loved to talk about his exploits in those entertainment venues through our coaching sessions. So, Michael decided to let the customer brag about those exploits and then listen attentively.

Michael would then visit the customer and ask how about a recent visit to the nightclub. The customer began to go into great detail about his exploits. Michael would then listen attentively, asking questions to clarify, and showed genuine interest in what the customer said for the next 15-30 minutes. Through it all, there wasn't any discussion about the business yet. However, the customer began to open up and communicate more with Michael. The subsequent business discussions became much smoother and more profound.

Perhaps the customer felt respected and appreciated. Maybe he felt the salesperson was someone he could talk to. Whatever it was, the rapport between the customer and the salesperson improved. On the other hand, Michael didn't have to entertain the customer in ways he didn't want or couldn't do.

One thing to note about applying tactical empathy in such situations is to refrain from making judgments. While the salesperson might disagree or even frown upon the customer's lifestyle, it is crucial that the salesperson does NOT pass judgment, but maintain curiosity about what the customer wants to discuss.

In this case, Michael found later on that this customer had some deeper personal issues. The decadent lifestyle was merely an escape for the customer from those unique challenges. Once again, Michael didn't do much, apart from showing empathy. After all, the customer's issues were too complicated for Michael to give any advice anyway.

He told the customer, "Sounds like you have a lot of issues to handle. Sorry I can't help much but thank you for sharing with me." To which the customer replied, "No need to say sorry. Thank you for listening."

It was a situation where the customer trusted the salesperson enough to show his vulnerable side to the salesperson. When we trust someone more, we are less defensive about our weaknesses and vulnerabilities. In this case, Michael won a high level of trust from the customer by drinking tea (not booze) and being an empathetic listener.

The key to building strong customer relationships is to build trust at both the business and personal levels. The key to building trust at both levels is to be empathetic. While it could be more challenging to build trust with some customers than others, demonstrating empathy is usually the first step to developing stronger relationships.

How to Sustain the customer's Interest in a Long Drawn Out Sales Cycle

If you have been selling B2B (Business-to-Business), you'd realize almost all of your sales are not concluded within 1 sales meeting. Typical industrial solutions sales cycles could range between 6-18 months. In some cases, it could be as long as 3 years.

The average length of the sales cycle will vary from industry to industry. In some cases, it could be 3 to 6 months. In others, it could be around a year or longer.

What can be determined is how early you are entering into the customer's buying process.

Sometimes we might approach customers when their need is not very clear. They might like your ideas and solutions, but it may be a while for them to define a need and perhaps raise a Request for

Proposal (RFP). The good thing about entering early in the sales cycle is that you have a "first-mover advantage" in shaping how the customer perceives an ideal solution or even how they map out their RFP.

The disadvantage of approaching the customer very early in the sales cycle is it will take much longer before you can get the sale, even if the customer is really interested in buying from you. Your greatest challenge will then be how to sustain the customer's interest throughout the sales cycle.

5 Key Areas of Focus When Following Through

Perhaps the worst way of following through with customers is to ask them "are you ready to sign the contract now" every time you follow through with them. While asking for the order is important, it is just as important to guide your customer to the purchase throughout the sales cycle.

Here are the 5 key steps you could and should take in the meantime.

1. Strategic Business Developments

- When you approach the customer at the early part of the sales cycle, you may want to focus your communications on broader issues rather than specifics of the purchase. This is because the customer might not have defined their needs, and is exploring various possibilities.
- Hence, you could take this opportunity to

understand a bit more about the customer's business and their strategic developments for the next 1-3 years.

2. Project Specific Developments

- When you are nearer to the customer's buying decision, you can now go into the specifics of their needs, particularly how your solution can be made to deliver results for the customer.
- You can help the customer compare the costs, benefits, and risks associated with the different options and guide the customer to make a decision they are comfortable with.

In this area, you could:

- Summarise what you had been discussing with the customer so far,
- Address if there are changes or additions to the customer's needs,
- Address any concerns the key stakeholders might have,
- Suggest ways to make your solutions work better, and
- Suggest subsequent action steps.

3. Technical Areas

- Depending on how early you enter the sales cycle, you can discuss various technical details with your customer. If you meet a customer in the earlier part of the sales

cycle, you can discuss technological trends and emergent developments. This will allow the customer to explore what could be optimal technical solutions to their needs.
- On the other hand, if you are at the latter part of the sales cycle, you then need to focus on specific technical issues. You probably need to do technical demos, tests, or analyses to prove your technical solutions work.

4. Personal Relationship Development

- While a B2B purchase is likely to be more rational than a B2C one, there will always be an emotional aspect of buying decisions. Besides the technical and business aspects, customers want to feel safe about the buying decision. As such, they would want to buy from someone they trust, i.e. someone they feel is reliable and can count on.
- Hence, regardless if you are at the earlier or latter part of the sales cycle, it makes sense to cultivate trusting relationships with customers. This could be done by fulfilling promises you made or proposing truly beneficial solutions to the customer.
- In addition, the more you know each other on a personal level, the higher the level of personal trust. So, if you can take time to learn the customer's personal history, family situation, or outlook on life, it will help build mutual trust. Similarly, the more a customer knows about you as a person, the

higher likelihood the customer will trust you more.

5. Organisation Mapping

- Besides having a longer sales cycle, the other key difference between B2B vs. B2C sales is there are more people involved in the buying decision in the former.
- If you foresee that it will be some time before you can complete the sale, one good way of following through is to find out more about the key stakeholders in your customer's organization.

You could find out:

- What roles do each key stakeholder play in the buying decision?
- What are some things each of them wants to achieve and some things each wants to avoid?
- What is each stakeholder's attitude towards you vis-à-vis the competition?
- What are the internal relationships between the stakeholders?
- In what sequence should you approach your stakeholders so you improve your chances of success?

As you can see from the above, there are quite a few things to do when following through with the customer. The next question then is: Would it be worth your while spending precious time and resources to do all these follow-through actions with your customer?

One critical step to take is to make sure you continuously qualify the customer or the sales opportunity. Sometimes it can be very difficult to make a good assessment if the sales opportunity is worth pursuing when you are in the very early part of the sales cycle. If you do feel it's not an opportunity worth pursuing anymore, perhaps you can respectfully tell the customer and see if they have other sales opportunities sometime in the future. On the one hand, if you find yourself progressing and advancing the sale, that is usually a good sign.

On the other hand, if you find this is one sales opportunity you need to follow through well, you will need to leverage as many aspects as possible to sustain the customer's interest throughout the sales cycle.

A Question of Trust

It is often said customers buy from people they like. While we don't usually buy from people we dislike, this old saying has one more dimension.

Customers Buy from People They Trust

To illustrate this point further, let's look at how a typical prospective customer reacts to new salespeople making the first contact with them (otherwise known as cold-calling):

- They find an excuse to hang up the phone as soon as possible.
- They make themselves very busy during appointments with sales people.
- They keep their mouths shut as much as possible when sales people ask questions.
- They will not refer the sales people to a higher authority even when such a need is clear.
- They often use delay tactics such as "If there is a need, we will call you" to appease sales people.

The reason customers don't trust salespeople is very simple: they feel the only thing salespeople care about is getting their money. Sadly, this "lust for the customers' money" is quite true with many salespeople out there, AND customers can smell them from miles away.

When customers make purchases, what they want in exchange for the money they spend is substantiated value. That is, can the products or services they buy bring better profits, reduce costs or simply improve their quality of life?

We could thus refer to the trust equation:

$$\text{TRUST} = \frac{\text{Credibility} + \text{Reliability} + \text{Intimacy}}{\text{Self Orientation}}$$

For a more detailed explanation of the above equation:

- Credibility – The level of expertise, clarity, and honesty, as perceived by the customer. This is mainly derived from the customer's experience of you as a person, although your qualifications or certifications might help a bit.
- Reliability – The level of dependability and consistency as perceived by the customer. This perception tends to be built up over multiple interactions and may require hard work to create a new customer relationship quickly.
- Intimacy – The extent the customer feels you are emotionally engaged with the issues they face, rather than just seeing them as a source of revenue. Intimacy exists when customers are willing to talk to you about complex issues and could be fostered by frequent, meaningful communications with the customer.
- Self-orientation – This is the extent to which the customer perceives you are thinking about your targets, fears, and desires rather than theirs. It can result from pushing for the sale regardless of whether the customer feels assured that they can benefit from your solutions.

Hence, the first step to build trust is this: You have to be perceived as being on the customers' side and proactively help solve customers' problems.

Here's a simple example. When most salespeople approach their prospective customers, they will say something like, "Hello, my name is XYZ, and I'm from ABC company. How are you today? I would like to show you a demo of our latest productivity-enhancing gadget. As I will be around your vicinity on Tuesday afternoon, can I come and see you around 2 p.m. or 4 p.m.?"

The problem with this approach is how these intended customers respond. They will either just say "not interested", or say yes and then get their secretaries to tell you "the boss has an urgent meeting, please leave your materials on the front desk, and we will call you when we have a need".

The reason for such responses from customers is they don't trust what you say. They probably have seen just too many "productivity-enhancing gadgets", and hear too many "I happen to be just in your neighbourhood" stories. Certainly, I will be too busy to meet just another peddler of gadgets. Furthermore, they don't trust you enough to tell you their "productivity" challenges if that is what your product will solve. Salespeople and their managers would have to work together to build trust and allay customers' fears that they will be taken advantage of or waste their time.

Instead, you can phrase your opening statement with something that's of value to the customer, such as:

"Hi, my name is c.j.. I understand many companies in your industry are facing serious challenges due to the sharp increases in raw material costs. Will you be open to exploring possible alternatives that might help improve your productivity and thereby reduce your costs?"

Perhaps the biggest destroyer of trust is to "over-promise and under-deliver". The causes of this destruction are two-fold:

- Salespeople make promises to customers about things they cannot (or are unsure if they can) deliver, and
- Companies that deliver less-than-expected levels of product quality to their customers.

In the former, sales managers would have to ensure salespeople do not over-promise their customers to get the sale or reach their sales target. Doing so will severely damage the trust between buyer and seller and make it more difficult for future sales efforts to succeed.

For the latter, nothing de-motivates salespeople more than answering customers' questions for which they don't have answers. No sales effort will succeed if the company does not invest enough in quality to make sure customers get the value they pay for. When companies deliver shoddy quality, not only will there be decreases in sales, there will also be an immediate increase in sales staff turnover. It's not a question of "if", it's just a question of time. After all, who wants to sell for a company they cannot trust?

Are You a Peddler or a Trusted Adviser?

The term for selling in Chinese can be sometimes termed as 推销, which means to peddle. It can also be 销售, which means simply making a sale. Still, the general perception is that one has to push products and services to customers to sell.

However, the most successful salespeople are masters in gaining the customer's trust and being trusted advisers. This is a complete departure from the traditional sales mindset where the salesperson is perceived as someone whose job is done by doing whatever it takes to push a product to a customer, collect the money, and run!

The best salespeople serve the best interests of BOTH their customers and the companies they work for, and then innovatively propose solutions all parties can benefit and accept. They act as consultants (at times unpaid) for their clients and make recommendations regarding what is best for customers (as opposed to their own pockets). They are willing to sacrifice the short-term sale if it's not the best solution for their customers, so they can win customers' hearts, minds, and souls in the long term.

Part 3

How to Sell to Customers When They Don't Have an Obvious Need?

I was looking for solutions to manage my team in Shanghai, not too long ago, while I was in Singapore. I have a great team, and I was looking for possible solutions to make the management process smoother.

I chanced upon a digital marketing agency that was promoting their "remote sales team" management services. I went to their website to get more information, and was told I needed to fill in an automated 22-question online survey. Some of the questions caught my attention for the wrong reasons, such as:

- "To what extent has remote working arrangements disrupted your day-to-day operations?"
- "How urgent is your problem?"
- "In your own honest opinion, what is preventing you from hitting your revenue goal?"

Indeed, in many sales training methodologies and handbooks, we are told to find out:

- What are the customers' problems?
- What are the implications if the problems are not resolved?
- What are the benefits if those problems are resolved?

While it is in the salesperson's interest to uncover the customer's pertinent and urgent needs, how those questions are phrased could positively or negatively impact the relationship.

Of great importance, Asian customers would like to save face. Even when they have some urgent needs, they probably would not want to admit anything negative or problems about themselves to a stranger, much less from an automated survey. Exploiting the customer's weaknesses on your first contact (such as asking "what's your problem?") is a sure way of dampening the relationship.

Even when your customers have a thick skin (like myself), they might not face any catastrophe if a need is not fulfilled. In my case, I definitely didn't have a problem. I was looking for solutions that could give me better results!

In addition, customers could have a hidden or future need, which needs to be explored with the salesperson. However, to do so, customers would explore such hidden or future needs only when there is strong mutual trust between buyer and seller. Asking questions that make the customer uncomfortable too early in the relationship is unlikely to increase mutual trust.

In some B2B cases, customers could be delighted with their current supplier. They just need to source a reliable 2nd or 3rd supplier due to compliance requirements in their companies.

Finally, some customers may not want to reveal their most dire need from a negotiation perspective for fear of diluting their bargaining power.

So, if we don't ask customers if they have "problems", what else can we do?

The Yin and Yang and Selling

Most people will think of Yin and Yang as day and night, positive and negative. In our case, however, we borrow the concept of Yin and Yang from Chinese martial arts or Taoism.

Whereas Yang in martial arts refers to the hard, pro-active and aggressive (or assertive) styles, Yin refers to flexible, empathetic and receptive ones.

An example of misusing the Yang way of selling is the traditional aggressive sales person who would force his products and services directly at customers, and not stop unless some cash (usually a big amount) is squeezed out of the customer. Generally, they:

- Don't take "no" for an answer,
- Likes to wow you with their product features and benefits, so you can't say no, and
- Will disappear the moment you make the payment, not appearing again until it's time to re-order.

However, suitable applications of the Yang type of selling could be:

- Taking the initiative to make things happen,
- Guiding and influencing customers' thinking,

- Asking questions to find out hidden needs and agenda,
- Navigating through different stakeholders and influencers that could have an impact on the final buying decisions,
- Being persevered to follow through long sales cycles,
- Not be discouraged by rejections, or when customers say "no",
- Overcoming objections and winning over customers,
- Working through and influencing internal colleagues to give the customers what they want,
- Doing whatever it takes to meet sales targets.

When facing rejection, salespeople can be assertive in the following ways:

- Persevering and following up with the customer over the long term,
- Not be discouraged by rejection, and move on to other, more suitable customers.

By and large, Yang salespeople are assertive enough to reach out to different existing and prospective customers. They would have to take actions to drive their ideas across and risk possible rejection and stalemates along the way. In complex sales situations, Yang salespeople would proactively reach out to different stakeholders and influencers that could impact the final buying decisions.

On the other hand, with increasing customer demands for salespeople to be more attentive to needs, there is now growing needs for the Yin salesperson. Yin salespeople are more attentive to customers' needs, and seek ways to fulfill those needs. The Yin salesperson might do things such as:

- Listen attentively to what customers say, as well as what they did NOT say,
- Build trust with customers,
- Be mindful of the customers' feelings and avoid antagonizing the customer,
- Have a positive "can do" attitude and provide great service.

Having empathy does not mean being nice to customers, or not saying "no" to customers. It simply means stepping into the shoes of customers, and seeing things from their point of view.

If the Yang salesperson is overly assertive and lacks enough empathy, they could become aggressive and offend customers. Sometimes Yang sales people may start by asking customers "Do you need...?" and are very likely to get a "NO" reply. When the salesperson pushes too hard, customers are more likely to push back and respond with direct rejection.

On the other hand, if the salesperson over-empathizes but is not assertive enough, they may lose control of the sales process and be pushed around by customers. Striking a balance between

Winning the B2B Sale in China

Yin and Yang styles of selling is critical.

Here's a typical scenario of how salespeople need to balance assertiveness and empathy in sales.

Let's say you have a prospective customer you are trying to build a relationship with. They tell you they are pretty happy with the current suppliers they have right now and do not need to buy from a new one.

A less assertive salesperson might just walk away. A salesperson who is all Yang but less Yin would try to convince the customer how the new products or solutions will deliver much better performances. However, the customer might perceive this as overly aggressive sales behaviour and, as such, become defensive. The customer might then avoid the salesperson in the future.

A sales person who has a balance of Yin and Yang could explore with the customer with questions such as:

- "Is it OK for us to explore alternatives?"
- "What kinds of support would you like to have to achieve your goals?"
- "What are some areas you would like to see improved? How is that important for you?"
- "Who else in your organisation would like to see improvements?"
- "If you are to work with an additional supplier (instead of changing suppliers), what would be some of your selection

criteria?"

In addition, Instead, salespeople can add value to the relationship by:

- Being responsive by pro-actively identifying current and potential challenges the customer may face, as well as suggesting ways the customer can overcome such challenges,
- Developing win-win relationships with multiple stakeholders or influencers so decision-makers don't have to sell your products and services internally to their colleagues,
- Being resourceful or even creative to work across different departments or business units to provide customized solutions that fit the customers' every need, and
- Being a reliable and trusted source of information and provider of reliable products and services.

Do note that in the initial phases of selling, the balanced sales person will avoid asking questions such as:

- "What kinds of products do you need?"
- "How much volume do you need?"
- "What price is good for you?"
- "When would you be buying?"

While these are indeed questions important to the salesperson, the customer has yet to trust the salesperson enough to provide such information. Neither are they yet interested in what the salesperson has to offer.

In other words, salespeople will be more successful if there is a good balance in the Yin and Yang of selling, especially in cases when there is no obvious need.

Qualifying Your Customers

The R&D people in Richard's customers' organisations lapped up the offer enthusiastically, even proactively asking Richard to provide more technical support so the new products could be developed quickly.

Unfortunately, when Richard's customer presented the new, revolutionary product to the customer's customer, the latter responded with "It's great, but we need to make this cheaper." This same feedback was then passed on to Richard, who was then asked by his customer to reduce his price significantly.

However, after spending lots of time and resources working with the customer's R&D to create this new product for the customer jointly, Richard's company could not reduce the price as they had to recover the cost of this initial investment. Besides, what Richard provided to the customer was already a high-end, revolutionary technology, which should not be given away at low prices.

Richard was frustrated and devastated. After spending months helping the customer, ultimately, he could not make the sale, with price being the main reason. Richard was now contemplating whether he should go and sell cheaper products and solutions instead.

Perhaps one of the most precious resources a sales person can have is time. A salesperson typically spends at most 30% of the average work day meeting with customers face-to-face. The rest of the time is either spent on traveling, internal meetings or doing admin work.

This means that salespeople can waste their precious time on poor prospects who are unlikely to buy, or they can focus their energies on qualified prospects who could eventually become paying customers.

At the same time, experienced salespeople are acutely aware they should spend more time with non-Purchasing or non-procurement people in the customers' organisations, such as R&D or Engineering or Production. This is to ensure they get deeper insights about the customers' needs, and even help identify hidden needs where the salespeople could add value.

However, not all customers are worth spending quality time with. Some customers are not targeted or qualified ones, and would not eventually make a purchase. This could be due to mismatches in terms of needs, technology, price, or even market segment. Instead of winning over the so-called tough customer, salespeople might be better off by focusing on customers whose needs and profile matches more of what the salespeople can offer and for which they could add value.

While a growing number of sales people are working closely with the customer's R&D department to jointly create the next-generation product for the customer's customer, these new products eventually got rejected by the customer's customer, citing high price as the main objection.

Although some of the customer's ultimately, objections can be resolved in different ways, perhaps salespeople would need to take the initial step of qualifying the customer's customer. If the salesperson is proposing a revolutionary next-generation product, and the customer's customer is focusing on the low-end market, that might not be a good match. While this could be true except in some exceptional circumstances where that customer is really committed to re-position themselves as a higher-end player in their markets. While such cases do happen occasionally, it would take a lot of courage and commitment for that customer to make the transition.

Another common mistake that salespeople tend to make when qualifying customers is to emphasize way too much about the expected sales volume. While volume is an essential criterion to evaluate if a particular customer should be given more attention, better services, or lower prices, other vital areas of consideration should include:

- Can the customer pay on time?

- Can you sell at a price that is still profitable to your company?

- Do you have healthy relationships with the key stakeholders of your customer? Etc.

Developing Customer Relationships in Technical Sales

Raymond was feeling very frustrated. He was once the company's best engineer, and was transferred to become a sales engineer because of his seemingly good people skills. Since Raymond enjoyed dealing with people just as much as doing his engineering work, he accepted the challenge. After all, he could potentially make more money, not to mention having the chance to progress exponentially in his career.

However, after some months into his work, he found he faced some unexpected challenges such as:

- Despite proposing what was objectively the best solution for the customer based on the customer's needs, the customer eventually decided to buy something that was in some ways inferior,
- Despite being willing to share with his customers all his professional technical knowledge, some customers simply aren't

interested in understanding the features and benefits of what they were buying,
- Despite getting very positive feedback from a customer, that customer changed their minds at the last minute.

To be fair to Raymond, he had been through some excellent sales training programmes. So, he's very proficient in asking questions and understanding customers' needs. He was also consciously aware of not overwhelming the customer with too many technical details and focusing on the critical value and benefits instead.

Still, Raymond felt like he had hit a brick wall, and was feeling very discouraged. He even thought of quitting his job, and join another company as an engineer again, even though he liked his current company.

So, what went wrong?

One of the key things many engineers don't (consciously) realize is: dealing with people is actually quite different from dealing with machines.

When you deal with a machine or equipment, if you have the same inputs and the same processes, you will get the same output every single time. If you don't, then there's something wrong with the machine.

However, having the same input and processes is unlikely to give you the same response whenever you deal with people. This unpredictability is the nature of human beings and is somewhat contrary to the expectations of many technical people.

Hence, even when the technical sales engineer could be very outgoing and enjoy dealing with people, they might not consciously realize that customers can give unpredictable responses.

What this means to technical sales people is:

- Customers can be right, even when you know they are wrong.

This is something many technical professionals find hard to accept. However, if they know the reasons behind such seemingly irrational customer behaviours, they could then use their analytical abilities to improve their sales performance.

In addition to analyzing the technical needs of the customer, technical sales people could examine some of the "buyer" oriented factors as well, including:

- Will there be negative consequences if customers don't make a purchase?
- Is the customer's evaluation criteria favorable to the seller's success?
- Does the seller understand the customer's buying decision process?
- Does the customer have the proper budget to fund this purchase?
- Is this a reasonable time frame and revenue to pursue this sale?
- What is the level of resistance of the key

buying influencers?
- What is the level of the relationship strength of our competition with the customer?
- What is the level of solution strength of our competition?

Hence, it's no surprise that one of our IT clients commented their top salespeople tend to be former pre-sales consultants who leaped into a sales position.

Part 4

Managing Your Relationships With Key Stakeholders

Winning the B2B Sale in China

A prospective customer's Technical Director approached David to develop better alternative solutions. The customer's current supplier had caused a massive delay in their production schedule, resulting in many customer complaints. As a result, the customer sent their Technical Director to look for alternative solutions from an alternative supplier. As the company David was working for had a solid reputation in terms of product quality, he was approached to be the alternative supplier.

While the samples David gave the customer showed David's products had surpassed the Technical Director's expectations and would prevent similar adverse incidences from happening, their senior management was still undecided after a few weeks.

What would you do if you were in David's situation?

It turns out the Technical Director was NOT the key decision-maker. So perhaps David should try to navigate his way to gain access to the key decision-maker and then make his case? Well, David did try to gain access, and for some reason, he only got a lukewarm reception from the customer's Managing Director.

To understand what happened, we would have to see things from the customer's angle. The customer, in this case was a typical entrepreneurial private enterprise in China. The founder was the Managing Director, the Finance Director was his wife, and the Purchasing Director his wife's brother.

As per any typical entrepreneur in China, the Managing Director was shrewd in haggling for the best prices from his suppliers, to the extent some of the suppliers were found to provide consistent product quality. Hence, once in a while, those suppliers would create some serious quality issues。 In this case, it had an immense impact on the customer.

The Managing Director was furious and wanted to change suppliers immediately. That was how their Technical Director was dispatched to look for David. However, this news quickly reached the current supplier, and just like any supplier, they would not lose the business without putting up a fight. They went to see the Managing Director, apologized profusely, promised compensation, and made guarantees such things would not happen again in the future. More importantly, they gave the Managing Director a significant discount to what was already a meager price.

With such an offer in hand, it was not surprising the Managing Director was not keen to work with David despite David surpassing the technical requirements. The reduction in prices from the current supplier was too alluring, and they "guaranteed" such adverse incidences would not happen again.

Furthermore, the Managing Director worked with this supplier for years and was unwilling to change suppliers. Perhaps David could alleviate the problems created by the current supplier, but would there be other unknown problems David's company could be creating? Like many other B2B buyers, the Managing Director would prefer to work with existing suppliers rather than take on unknown risks to new ones, especially when the current supplier gave a considerable discount to retain the business.

By the time David told me this story, he had lost the deal to the customer's current supplier. However, was there anything else he could have done?

As I coached David further, we explored the issue of "who would hurt the most should the supplier cause quality problems again?" We found there was someone that fit the description and was left out of the earlier discussions. The customer's Sales Director would be at the forefront of bearing the brunt of massive customer complaints and losing customers due to their supplier's folly. It also turned out that, unlike the Technical Director who was hired because of good technical skills but otherwise was considered an "outsider", the Sales Director was a cousin of the Managing Director's wife. He was capable and had good trust within the Managing Director's family.

If only David had thought about the Sales Director and tried to win him over. David could have elaborated that it was improbable the current supplier could ensure any form of consistent quality with a ridiculously low price, especially when they were producing in large batches. It was a matter of "when" and not "if" the next massive quality issue would happen with that supplier. When such cases occur again, the Sales Director would be inflicted with a stream of complaints, rejected products, and lost customers.

However, if the customer could purchase from David, such issues would be reduced to a minimum. Even though the prices David's company charged were significantly higher, it was comparatively less costly than having to lose customers, make refunds and tarnish one's reputation.

As David had moved on with other customers, he didn't follow up with that customer's Sales Director. While that particular customer certainly brought some interesting stories, they didn't qualify as a potential key account for David, and David simply went on to serve other customers who were more profitable but less dramatic.

Keep Your Friends Close

As Michael Corleone said in Godfather II: "Keep your friends close, and your enemies closer". This was great advice for relationship selling. Perhaps not so much about the "enemies" part of the quote, but more so on the "friends' part.

Some research claimed that in many cases, B2B salespeople would have to deal with 3 or more key contact persons or key buying influencers to win the sale. In our experience in China, sometimes that number could range between 5 to 7 key people.

Depending on the industry, some of the key buying influencers could be external partners of the customer. In the construction and building industry, for instance, key buying influencers would include the architects and the main contractor for construction projects.

As the Chinese saying goes, 有人的地方就有江湖 or where there are people there will be complex relationships. Having friends within the customer's organization will be a great help while navigating through these complex and sometimes conflicting relationships. On the outside, we view the customer as a monolith where they make the eventual unified decision to buy or not to buy from you. Internally, though, different influencers within the customer's organization might have different agendas pulling in different directions.

Having a friend within the customer's organization is akin to what ancient Chinese say as 朝中有人, or you have a supporter in the imperial court. Having this supporter within the customer's organsation will allow you to:

- Get information about what is happening within the customer's organization,
- Gain access to the right people to influence their buying decisions, and
- Ask your supporter to influence others by highlighting your strengths and give assurances at appropriate times.

In one particular case years ago, one of our trainees claimed he could know:

- How much inventory his company had with a specific customer, vis-a-vis the inventory his competitor had,
- What share of purchase this customer was buying from him, vis-a-vis the competitor, and
- Inventory movements from his company and the competition in and out of the customer's logistics facilities, faster than the customer's SAP system.

How did he accomplish this? By making friends with the warehouse manager, of course!

What is important here is not so much about how many people you need to win over, but more about how you could fulfill each of their needs as much as you can, hence the premise "keep your friends close".

As far as the second half of the phrase "keep your enemies closer" is concerned, the application is limited in sales. While there could be detractors and opposition in the customer's organisation, usually, these are seldom people with a personal vendetta against you. They typically have very rational reasons to doubt you, your solutions, or even your company. Sometimes it could be a matter of winning them over, rather than treating them as "enemies".

However, there are times that such detractors and

opposition may not reveal their true intentions in public, especially in your presence. Hence, detractors and opposition could appear warm and welcoming to you but immediately shoot down your proposals the moment you turn your back. The more significant challenge is you probably wouldn't know who the detractors are unless your friends know and inform you about it. Hence the emphasis on "keep your friends" close, and hopefully, they share important information with you!

Selling Without Knowing the Key Decision Makers

There are many times a sale is made without ever seeing the key decision-makers. Some decision-makers make buying decisions behind closed doors and refuse any interactions with salespeople. Others take a more passive role, preferring to veto if they feel a particular buying decision is not right but otherwise taking a passive approach towards buying decisions.

However, key decision makers rarely make decisions in a vacuum. They most probably would seek input from their lieutenants, who could be buying influencers. They have a certain amount of influence to shape how buying decisions are made in their respective organizations.

Each buying influencer has a job role or a persona. Each persona of a specific job role would have particular issues they are concerned about, such as:

- <u>Purchasing managers</u>: Manage total

purchasing expenditure and mitigate organizational risks.
- <u>Engineering managers</u>: Quality, Costs, and Delivery (QCD).
- <u>Operations/ production managers</u>: Productivity, process quality, and responding to changes in specifications.
- <u>Finance managers</u>: Mitigate financial risks, compliance to regulations, and improve financial performance.
- <u>Sales managers</u>: Achieve revenue and gross margin targets while ensuring customer retention.
- <u>Top management</u>: Strategic development of the company.

One thing to note is that while purchasing managers are concerned with managing purchasing expenditure, that may not always mean bargaining for a lower unit price. While you may not be necessarily offering the lowest unit price, purchasing managers could still manage or reduce expenditure if they could:

- Buy lesser quantities,
- Incur less maintenance,
- Reduce replacement of parts, and
- Reduce the number of replacements.

In addition, purchasing managers are also very much concerned about on-time deliveries and consistency of quality. If anything were to go wrong, purchasing managers expect salespeople to respond to their requests for assistance immediately.

Hence, while purchasing managers are cost-conscious, there is also an underlying need to trust the salesperson in times of need.

When keeping friends close, salespeople would need to be clear about what each persona in the customers' organization needs and seek ways to fulfill those needs. More importantly, salespeople need to know what buttons to press to obtain the right responses from different buying influencers.

The Customer's Customer

Sometimes, the customer buys from a supplier solely because the customer's customer had specifically appointed that supplier to be the upstream supplier. Many salespeople understand the significance of the customer's customer. However, reaching out and influencing that customer's customer is usually more complex.

It is unusual and strange for the salesperson to reach out directly to the customer's customer. It is thus more likely the salesperson reaches out to the customer's salespeople to understand more about their customer's needs and concerns.

Hence, while it is commendable and essential salespeople reach out to the customer's R&D and Engineering departments to influence them to buy, it is another thing altogether if the customer's customer would accept the end-product at the price all parties are agreeable to. As such, salespeople might be required to include the customer's customer as a buying influencer and seek direct or indirect ways to make friends with them!

Making Friends with Different Types of Customers

So far, we have been discussing making friends with customers and keeping friends close. The question is, does your customer treat you as a friend as well? What if some of them don't?

Managing the different types of key accounts

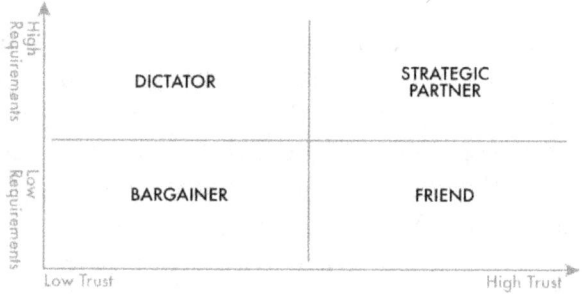

We can have customers classified into the following four combinations:

- High-Requirements vs. Low-Requirements
- High-Trust vs. Low-Trust Customers

"Requirements" can be:

- The technical complexity of the product,
- Customer knowledge of the product,
- Customer confidence in understanding his/her needs.

Suppose a product is complex and the customer does not understand the product's performance, technology, or applications. In that case, the customer has to rely on the salesperson to guide the customer into the most effective solution.

However, suppose the product is technically complex, and the customer is well-versed in those complexities. In that case, he will tend to ask salespeople to follow and implement his ideas and demands strictly.

If customers are gradually familiar with complex products' technical and application aspects, these products will become less complex over time. For example, in the 1980s, desktop computers were considered a very sophisticated high-tech device, and customers needed the guidance of salespeople to find one that suited their needs. Later, however, when the customer had become more knowledgeable about computers, and while the functionalities of the products had become more complex as years went by, customers were very much able to do their computer shopping online without the assistance of salespeople.

In addition, the customer also needs to understand the operational and business aspects associated with purchasing the product. The more customers become knowledgeable, the more demanding they become, hence the higher requirements they need.

Customers who are not knowledgeable will usually only be concerned about some of the more superficial issues, such as price, payment terms, and popularity of the supplier. More knowledgeable customers tend to be more concerned about efficiency, the total cost of ownership, business fit, and other factors.

In addition to identifying "High Requirements" and "Low Requirements" customer situations, the salesperson should also be able to determine which customers are more open to discussing future possibilities, needs, and challenges, as well as which customers are more closed to such discussions.

The more open customer will be willing to share their ideas and challenges with salespeople, including specific requirements, questions, budgets, concerns, and so on. Customers who trust the salesperson less will be reluctant to share information or initiate contact.

Customers with Low Requirements and Low Trust tend to focus more on the "Bargainer" persona and be more price sensitive. This customer manages to squeeze prices with salespeople, especially using high-volume promises in exchange for lower prices. And even when the salesperson wants to offer a better solution, they will be subject to customers' questions and resistance.

For such customers, salespeople need to gain their trust gradually and then let them know how to reduce the overall cost of procurement (Total Cost of Procurement).

Some of the "Bargainer" customers may seem more knowledgeable and actually might be "pretending to know when they don't know". This behavior could be due to the customer's distrust of the salesperson and the complexity of the product technology or procurement requirements. Hence, they are reluctant to share with salespeople they barely know about how little they understand. When dealing with such customers, salespeople may want to find others these customers trust and then influence these customers indirectly.

If the salesperson aims to persuade and influence the customer, they have to find the "Friend" type of customer. These customers know they have a limited understanding of what they want to buy, and they are willing to take further action to learn and understand. They are not limited to understanding the needs of the purchase and related requirements. Instead, they need to do everything they can to communicate with their business, technology, and user-related departments to understand their needs. Such customers will be grateful to the salespeople who are willing to spend time and impart knowledge and insights.

"Dictators" know what they are doing and will exert their decisiveness and dominance. They will give clear instructions to salespeople, and if the salespeople were to give counter-suggestions, they would be seen as giving excuses instead. When facing "Dictator" customers, salespeople need to be very diligent and dedicated to meeting customers' demanding requirements. They also have to be consistent in both performance and service, so the "Dictator" customer could grow to trust their abilities.

Although the "Dictator" may be very knowledgeable and understand the technology, they will not always know everything. They will also make subjective, judgmental errors. When selling to the "Dictator", the salesperson needs to do a lot of related preparation, be prepared to be challenged with many pointed questions, and handle those sharp questions convincingly.

Finally, there's the "Strategic Partner". This type of customer is rare. They are demanding, and they also need a salesperson they trust to help them achieve their goals. "Strategic Partners" often emphasize long-term relationships and require the seller to customize the formatting services.

However, this does not mean all "Strategic Partner" customers are good customers as they tend to consume a lot of time, energy, and resources. Salespeople will need to assess whether investments in time and resources are worth the results eventually given by those customers.

Even when salespeople can identify whether customers are "Bargainer" or "Strategic Partner" types, customers will change their behavior and thinking over time.

Here are some essential tips salespeople can use, even with the most demanding customers:

- Be prepared. Do not rush to a sales meeting unprepared. Be well-prepared to answer some tough questions and objections customers may hurl at you.
- Establish trust. Do not sell in a hurry. Take time to understand the customer's business, technology, needs, and concerns, so customers will want to understand your solution.
- Do not just rely on one contact person. Pay attention to those who claim to be key decision-makers, but in fact, are not. Often, key decision-makers do not say they are key decision-makers, and those who claim to be decision-makers are usually not. Develop good relationships with all key influencers in the buying decision.

When dealing with key customers, salespeople must know how to adapt to different customer attitudes and forge a path that will hopefully lead to good results.

Part 5

Relationship Pricing

Winning the B2B Sale in China

Some time ago, my friend Cathy saw an online ad for an international super-5-star hotel in Qingdao offering a very attractive promotion when China had just returned to a certain degree of normalcy from the Covid-19 outbreak in mid-2020. A night's stay that was selling at US$127 in the same period just a year ago is now sold at US$70 net, and they even threw in 2 international buffet breakfasts to boot. Since Cathy was making a trip in that general direction anyway, she thought she might as well take up the offer and booked 2 nights with her husband. This could well be a well-deserved post-Covid-19 mini-honeymoon.

Except that it was not the case. After staying in that hotel for 2 nights, Cathy said she would never stay in that hotel ever again! Among her list of complaints were:

- Due to the reduced number of hotel guests, the selection of dishes for the international buffet breakfasts was limited, and she'd rather eat out at the street vendors..
- Due to Covid-19 prevention, the swimming pool was not open, which was only mentioned in the fine print.
- The hotel was severely understaffed by very inexperienced staff, such that they could not even provide simple answers to guest inquiries.

After her "ordeal" with the hotel, Cathy summed it all up, saying that just because the hotel lowered their prices by a significant factor, that didn't mean customers would reduce their expectations. Instead, customers would maintain the same level of expectation, discounts or not.

There are times when the pressure from the customer and the competition to make you drop your prices is enormous, regardless of how strong your relationship is with your customer. Even when the customer is not asking for a discount, salespeople may feel compelled to offer great deals to entice the customer.

For the record, I am in no way saying we, as sellers, should not drop prices. Our humble consulting practices have also reduced rates in some circumstances.

I want to highlight that even when you drop prices to the extent you give away your product for free, customers will still retain the same level of expectation before you give any discounts.

While this can happen to the hospitality industry, as shown above, the same phenomenon applies to any industry and market. If sellers expect to deliver a lower standard due to the decrease in prices and customers, they will be in for a rude shock. Eventually, if sellers are not careful, they may win the sale at the expense of losing customers and tarnishing their brand.

So, if there's this enormous pressure to drop your price, and if you drop the price, you probably will not be able to deliver to the same levels of service or performance, how then do you deal with this situation?

Remember I mentioned my consultancy has also reduced our fees in certain circumstances? Here's what happened.

I have been facilitating many face-to-face workshops for many clients in China. Due to Covid-19 travel restrictions imposed by China and many other countries, at one point, I could not travel to China even with valid work visas. For the clients that require my services, I could only conduct online facilitation for them. To sweeten the deal, we could do a certain percentage mark-down on our fees if they feel online facilitation isn't quite the same as a face-to-face one.

In communicating customers' expectations, I already have gotten my customers to set lower expectations. They know I could not be with them in person. So, my lowering of fees was positioned as a gesture of understanding their concerns, and I responded accordingly.

Does that mean I would lower the quality of my delivery? Absolutely not! In one case, we had a client who didn't want us to reduce our fees. Instead, they required us to invest a lot of time together with them to go through various iterations of the online workshops to make sure the participants would get the best possible facilitation with an online version of me. In other words, while we are grateful to the client for not pushing for a lower rate, we worked our bums off by putting in extra hours to strive for perfection. Since they have been a great customer for many years, we gladly did so for them.

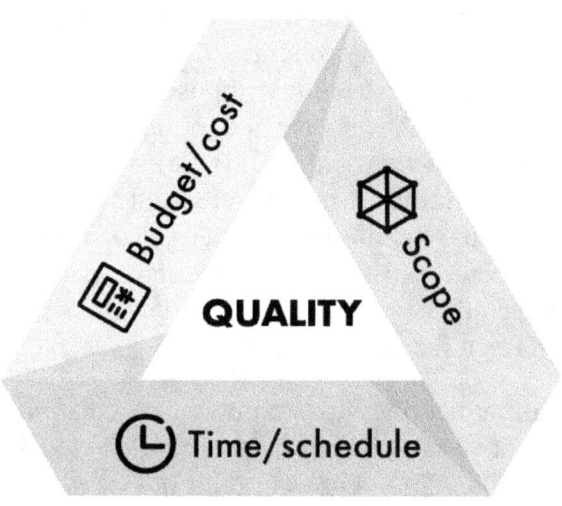

So, what does this imply for the rest of us? As a reduction in prices or budgets could mean there could be reductions in the scope of work or the quality being delivered, it may be wise to use these reductions as a bargaining chip with the customer.

In our case, it could be the fact that I couldn't be physically present with our customers, which I stated upfront. So, if your customer is pressuring you to reduce the price, you may ask to trade a reduction of price with some reduction in service or a longer delivery lead time. Put those trade-offs upfront so customers know full well they would have to adjust their expectations to enjoy a price saving.

In the context of the hotel example mentioned earlier, being upfront about the potential reduction of services provided might mean reducing the appeal of the price discount. Imagine the hotel putting an ad saying that:

""Enjoy 50% off our regular rate. Do note the selection at our otherwise sumptuous breakfast might be cut in half. So will our service staff. The pool is also not available."

It probably will not work that way. However, one can still put a positive spin by adapting the message into something like:

"Welcome to our new streamlined mode of operations to cope with the Covid-19 New Normal. Some of our usual services will be self-service, and the swimming pool is closed due to health restrictions. To make it up to you, we will be providing our room serviced breakfast set meals for all guests for free, AND we are giving 50% discount off our regular rates."

While such a rephrasing may not always work for all customers. At the very least, your brand and reputation will not be tarnished. You are likely to get customers to return, and even for those who choose not to buy now, you could still win them over when things resume back to normalcy!

Your Closest Customers Will STILL Ask for a Cost-Down!

While customers may not reduce their expectations just because you reduce your prices, most of your closest customers will still ask for discounts from time to time. Nobody wants to pay more than they have, and it's just natural for customers to see if they are getting a fair price from you. Sometimes, they do so by asking you to reduce your prices.

One common reason customers are asking for price reductions is due to the need for a "cost-down" for their purchases. Some purchasing managers even discuss with salespeople about the prices for the next number of years to factor in the cost-downs in the foreseeable future.

From the salesperson's perspective, though, there are times when you are unable to reduce prices any further. While some customers may understand and accommodate your situation, others might reduce their purchases or seek ways to phase out your products when prices cannot be reduced further.

What salespeople can do, though, is to explore with the customer to possibly help them achieve better costs without having to reduce prices. While this line of argument may not always work, it will be more likely to work if you have stronger relationships with the customer.

To understand this concept, you will need to help the customer understand the distinction between "price" and "costs". A simple way to illustrate that will be akin to buying a car, supposing you were reducing paid US$50,000/= for a car. The US$50,000/= is the price you paid, but is that the cost of owning and using the car? The answer is no. On top of your purchase price, you still need to pay for the fuel, parking, maintenance, and other associated expenses.

Your cost of owning the car will also need to take into consideration non-monetary costs. For instance, perhaps you bought this car at a real bargain, and they even gave you unlimited free parts and service maintenance for the next 5 years. It sounds like a good deal, right? However, what if the car breaks down and requires maintenance every few days? If that were to happen, even though the maintenance charges are free, you would still have to incur the opportunity costs of not having the car for the days when it breaks down.

Now, you could apply the same logic to your customer's situation. Although you could not reduce prices to match your competitor's, would you still be able to help your customer to:

- Reduce downtime or improve up-time,
- Ensure consistency of quality,
- Reduce maintenance costs,
- Reduce operational costs, and
- Improve productivity?

One of the leading companies in the chemical industry specifically trains their salespeople on how to justify the cost savings they provide despite selling at higher prices. The chemical product requires its manufacturing customers to heat it to a specific temperature to complete the manufacturing process. The product this chemical company is selling can be processed at 5 degrees Celsius lower than a main competing product.

So, one may think 5 degrees Celsius lower in terms of temperature is no big deal. Well, it turns out a reduction in heat generation of 5 degrees Celsius compounded over the quantities produced over a prolonged period would reduce the energy bill for the end customer. The chemical company calculated how much it would cost their customer to generate 1 degree Celsius of heat for the production capacity over 1 year. Their salespeople then presented such savings to convince their customers they help their customers to save costs over the year, despite their higher price.

Besides saving on energy costs, sometimes processing at lower temperatures could help customers dominate entire markets. Legend has it the dominant brand of cup noodles in China, Kangshifu or Master Kong, won about 47% of China's cup noodle market with one single selling point. Before China put on its High-Speed Rail system in the old days, train journeys could take a long time from city to city. Many passengers brought their cup noodles as refreshments along the way to soothe their hunger.

There was one problem though. Cup noodles need boiling water to heat them, and it's hard to get boiling water of 100 degree Celsius on the train. Typically, train attendants will boil water in a kettle and serve hungry passengers waiting eagerly with their cup noodles. Unfortunately, by the time the water was poured onto the cup noodles, the water temperature would have cooled to around 90 degrees Celsius. What Kangshifu did was innovate their noodles by making them possible to be cooked and soften at 10 degrees Celsius lower than the boiling point. With that one masterstroke, Kangshifu captured the Chinese cup noodle market!

Now, salespeople can share stories like these with customers. Whether customers are willing to buy into such stories would depend a lot on the relationship and trust with the salespeople. If the customer trusts you enough, you could still sell at a higher price as long as you can justify the project cost savings from using your products and solutions.

Are There Any Other Concerns Besides Price?

While price will always be a concern and often a key concern, customers are likely to have other concerns besides price. Although they might initially mention price reductions as a key demand, they might have other deeper concerns and objections they have yet to verbalize.

When customers hesitate to make a purchase, they could be having the following risk factor concerns besides price:

- What if there are hidden costs we don't

know about?
- What if it fails or does not work as promised?
- What if the after-sales service is not timely enough?

When customers raise concerns or objections like these, it is important for salespeople NOT to jump right in and make an explanation first. When salespeople are too quick to explain themselves, they could be perceived as defensive by customers, and the conversation could escalate quickly into a heated argument. What you want to do is find a mutually acceptable path so you can move forward and get on with your business. You do not want to prove yourself right and the customer wrong, as that could potentially damage your relationship resulting in a lose-lose outcome.

You can adopt the following steps to address the customer's concerns:

- <u>Affirm.</u> Let the other person know you are listening and can see things from their point of view.
- <u>Clarify.</u> Instead of rushing in to explain things, which may be perceived as defensive, ask questions to clarify what they meant.
- <u>Suggest.</u> Make your suggestions in the form of questions to explore options and co-create the solution with the other party.
- <u>Check.</u> Check whether the other party can accept the path forward and move on.

Hence, if the customer raises a price objection with you, you can start by asking:

- "Thank you for your feedback. I understand your concern."
- "When you say our price is high, how much higher is that from your expectation? May I understand how you arrived at this conclusion?"
- "What other concerns do you have besides price?"
- "If we can use other ways to help you save costs, would that be something you would like to explore?"
- "If we could prove to you your cost-savings is more than your expected price reductions, is that an acceptable outcome for you?"

Sometimes, the disagreements can be very complex and run on a much deeper level. When such deeper disputes happen, you may want to try the following 7 steps to resolve those deeper issues:

1. Establish a common goal or objective. If both the salesperson and the customer are heading towards the same objectives, then there is hope to resolve the differences.
2. Present the facts. Let each party present the facts as each side perceives them, without any prejudice. The critical thing here is about your ability to see things from the customer's point of view and vice versa..
3. Look for the positives. Instead of telling the customer, they are wrong, start by pointing

out the valid points the customer had shared. Being able to agree on just some of the issues can go a long way in resolving conflicts.

4. <u>Address mutual concerns</u>. It will not be a disagreement if there are no causes of concern. So, this is the time to share the key points of disagreement. Again, the key thing here is to listen and see things from the customer's point of view before making a judgment.

5. <u>Co-create new solutions</u>. When we raise concerns or differences to each other, it's not to put down the customer. Instead, what we'd like to do is help each other co-create mutually acceptable solutions. After all, it's a matter of different opinions or ways of working to reach a common goal.

6. <u>Empathize with each other</u>. If there are any solutions proposed at this juncture, be sure to check with your gut regarding how you feel about it. And allow the customer to check with their gut feelings too. Do check for signs of whether the customer is feeling positively or negatively about the proposed solution. If the customer's gut feeling is negative, they may not commit to the purchase in the end. You may then need to ask questions such as "Is there anything bothering you about this solution?" to see what other issues need to be resolved.

7. <u>Mapping the next steps</u>. Resolving complex disagreements like these is just the first step

of really getting things done together. The next step will be how both the salesperson and the customer map out moving forward and have milestones to check whether everything is on track.

One key element that is crucial to make the resolving of customers' concerns work is active listening. Customers want to be heard and feel they have your fullest attention. You will need to listen actively to the customer's perspectives, concerns, and other issues. The more you understand your customer, the more you will understand the issues and the greater likelihood of resolving them.

So, while your closest customers may still bring up the price issue with you, you will need to assess the contextual situation and communicate with them accordingly. If you have a trusting relationship with your customer, you have a much higher chance of mitigating their concerns and winning the sale. Some of these concepts can be pretty simple to understand but can take a lifetime to perfect. The more you practice these concepts, the better to co-create mutually agreeable solutions with your customers.

Part 6

Engaging With Internal Stakeholders to Fulfill External Customers' Needs

Winning the B2B Sale in China

Ted was under pressure to meet his sales targets by the end of the month, or he might be asked to leave the company. Fortunately for him, he met a customer who had shown great interest in the products and solutions he was selling and was keen to work with Ted's company for an upcoming project.

The customer gave a very tight deadline and was bargaining hard to bring the price down. Ted had to plead with his manager to approve special pricing, and his manager, not wanting to lose a team member, supported it.

Unfortunately, this was just the beginning of Ted's misery. Despite paying a very low price, the client kept adding specifications to Ted's company's solution. Ted had to be the coordinator between the customer's demands and the internal colleagues responsible for delivering the solution for the customer. As there was a resource crunch internally, Ted's colleagues could not provide sufficient support within the tight deadline set by the customer. The customer, in turn piled up the pressure on Ted, threatening to refuse payment if their demands were not met.

Ted had to escalate the situation internally, asking his manager to persuade the managers of his internal colleagues while he appeased the customer. Eventually, the solutions were delivered for the customer, and the customer made their payments.

However, Ted didn't emerge a winner through it all.

The customer felt Ted's company was slow in responding to their needs. Ted's colleagues found Ted to be overbearing and unreasonable and preferred not to work with him in the future. They particularly resented Ted for using their managers to add pressure on them. Ted's manager felt that Ted's inability to manage the customer's expectations led to increased tensions internally and cost overruns to fulfill the customer's requirements..

While Ted did manage to stay on with his company for the moment, he might not get the same level of support internally to serve future customers. Unless he can turn things around, he might still see his career at this company being cut short.

What is Negotiable and What Is Not

When you sell solutions that are part of a customer's project, there is a strong likelihood that the project would be affected by additional (and quite often, last-minute) customer requests. Or, due to reasons caused by the customer, the project is delayed, and you will need to add man-days to it.

Furthermore, if you ask for more fees to cover the additional work, some customers may complain to your management, to avoid paying more fees. To appease customers, some senior managers might agree with the customers, thereby putting the site supervisor in an embarrassing situation.

When customers start to make additional requirements, the first step to thinking about is what they are requesting, which are negotiable, and a firm "no".

Do note whenever there are additional requests, keep in mind the request will impact one or more of the following:

- Scope (i.e. deliverables),
- Resources required, and
- Time.

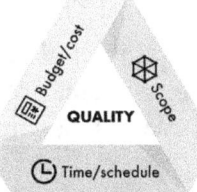

That is to say, with every additional scope (requirement) or request, it's likely to add demands for more resources or time or both. Hence for each further increase in scope, ask yourself if you can afford the additional time or resources. The next question to ask is: If you add more resources or time to the project, would that incur more costs, and will you need to charge more?

If the available time or resources are not available to add more scope, then the answer is "no". It is not a matter of being nice or nasty. However, instead, if there is a resource crunch, the request is therefore not negotiable.

On the other hand, when the additional time and resources are available for increased scope, it will be an issue of deciding if the customer needs to be charged for the extra time and resources given. Sometimes Project Managers may choose not to charge the customer if the costs incurred are manageable. However, if the scope keeps on creeping, it could also reach a point you have to charge additional fees. The only thing to negotiate will be "how much"?

Whether you decide to charge or not to charge extra fees, what needs to be done is to ensure you gain alignment internally.

Some things that will require alignment between site engineers, project managers, account managers, and even management may include:

- Can the project team cope with requests to increased scope in terms of available time and resources?
- How much to charge customers for the increased scope, and at what point?
- How will the communication be made with the customer? What will be the aligned message?

The reasons for gaining internal alignment before communicating with customers are to:

- Avoid customer confusion if there are different or conflicting messages communicated by other people from the salesperson's organisation, and
- Prevent the customer from pitting one stakeholder from the sales person's organization against another.

This is especially so for the latter, which customers may do, just to get what they want without paying.

Some salespeople or even senior customer-facing

managers might want to pressure their other colleagues to accede to customers' requests without compensation. While this could be a business decision where the objective is to retain the customer for potential future business, the key point is that such decisions need to be aligned internally.

The final decision could be to continue to fulfill additional customer's requirements:

- Without charge, for now, and ever,
- Without charge up until a certain extent, or
- Start charging the customer.

Whatever the consensus internally, those decisions must be explicitly clear to all project team members and communicate with customers.

Perhaps the key to gaining alignment internally is to ensure all parties communicate well with one another and keep one another informed about the latest updates regarding different aspects of the project. In most cases, project updates tend to focus on project progress status. Many times, some elements are not well-communicated, such as:

- Potential changes in customers' scope and requirements,
- Differences between customers' expectations and what will actually be delivered, and
- Availability of additional time or resources if the scope of the project is increased.

Many stories abound about how salespeople and

other internal colleagues could not get along well with one another and at times limit their communication internally. This could be detrimental to all parties. While some customers might simply exploit internal discord within the seller's organization to maximize their gains, eventually, they might end up with a less satisfactory final delivery. The customer might then choose to work with other suppliers in the future. Hence, such situations might be a lose-lose for both the customer and the sales person's organization if they do not handle it well.

Being Agile in Your Internal Communications

Perhaps when coordinating internally when customer situations are Volatile, Uncertain, Complex, and Ambiguous (VUCA), salespeople might want to adopt some agile methodologies to be flexible yet structured enough in internal communications.

Unlike situations where things are stable and predictable, one could not use step-by-step procedures to reach their goals, as shown in the diagram below:

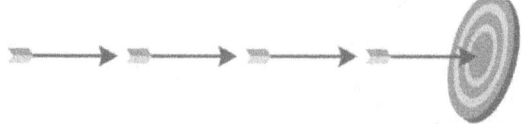

During a more turbulent situation, due to many unknown and emergent factors, one would have to take smaller steps and make adjustments along the way to reach goals.

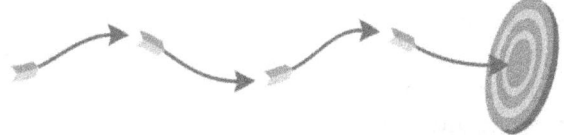

As a result, you can take smaller actions and make adjustments when you get more information or greater clarity.

To achieve agility, though, according to research by McKinsey's, agile organizations need to have:

1. Clear shared common vision and purpose.
2. A network of empowered teams with clear and flat organization structures.
3. Rapid decision-making and learning cycles.
4. Self-motivated and passionate people that support one another.
5. Evolving technology that supports business and team goals.

In other words, great sales people would have to sell internally and win over internal colleagues, just as they would with external customers.

During her work with a demanding customer, Margaret demonstrated her agile communication skills to gain buy-in from her colleagues to fulfill her customer's needs. Like every other demanding customer, this customer was asking for more things to add to the scope of work without extending deadlines and was unwilling to pay more.

Before even asking for help from her colleagues, Margaret managed her customer's expectations by prioritizing their requirements, categorizing them using the Moscow method:

- Must-have.
- Should-have.
- Could-have.
- Won't-have.

"Must-haves" are the things the customer must do or implement, or the whole project will fail. "Should-haves" are things that will give the customer a better result but can be omitted or postponed if time or resources are really tight.

"Could-haves" are things that would be nice to have but are not essential. "Won't-haves" are things that are not worthwhile to invest in time and resources at this juncture.

By going through this prioritization, Margaret found most of her customer's additional requirements are "Could-haves", with a few "Should-haves". She then let her customer understand that focusing on the "Could-haves" when the tight deadlines and limited budgets could only result in unnecessary delays and might eventually cause additional costs and damage.

While the customer agreed to shelve their "Could-have" requirements until later, they pushed Margaret to implement those requirements that fall under the "Should-haves" category. Margaret then decided to speak with her internal colleagues to see what could be done for the customer.

When Margaret got back to her company, she gave an update about the customer to all internal stakeholders who were working to deliver for the customer in one way or another. She made it clear she had reasoned with the customer, and there were specific additional requirements the customer felt strongly would have a significant impact on the final outcome.

As every salesperson would claim their customer is the most important customer, Margaret would have to present the facts to her colleagues and explain why this customer needed additional attention. As she had kept vital information such as the size of the deal and projected business with this customer over the next 12-24 months in her CRM, she was able to present objective information to convince her manager and colleagues to support her.

Together with her colleagues, Margaret wanted to establish the following information:

- How much work would be required if her colleagues were to help her fulfill those additional requirements,
- A workable schedule internally to deliver those additional requirements,
- Would Margaret's company need to charge the customer for the additional work, especially if the work was going to incur significant amounts of resources, and

- Could Margaret's company expedite the delivery of the additional requirements IF the customer was willing to pay extra for them?

Once she got the information from her internal colleagues, she went back and negotiated with her customer. The customer was adamant Margaret's company implement the additional requirements without extending deadlines and adding extra payments. Margaret made sure she conducted a principled discussion about what could be done, and the implications to the customer.

Eventually, the customer agreed to an extension of the deadline to have the additional requirements delivered without paying more. However, this was not the end of Margaret's work. She would have to influence her colleagues to ensure the requirements would be delivered based on the extended deadlines.

Now Margaret's story might sound pretty much a textbook definition of how salespeople could coordinate internally to meet customers' expectations. However, Margaret's ability to gain buy-in internally went well beyond her job scope to build mutual trust and respect with her colleagues,

Margaret built trust and respect with her colleagues by:

- Showing heartfelt appreciation whenever her colleagues helped her, no matter how small the assistance was,

- Refraining from making hurtful comments when her colleagues turned down her requests for help, and
- Refraining from saying any negative things about any colleague behind their back.

Margaret also demonstrated strong resilience when taking a principled approach to navigate her way internally and externally. She would have to coordinate or even mediate repeatedly between her customer and her colleagues so that all parties could find a mutually beneficial way forward. Fortunately for Margaret, her company has a customer-centric culture and strives to do what is best for the customer. Margaret's managers are also supportive towards her, primarily due to her diligence when dealing with complex customer issues.

The critical differentiator between great salespeople and mediocre ones would be how much the salesperson has a sense of self and how well the salesperson can regulate their emotions.

Great salespeople tend to be keenly aware of the contextual environment and what kinds of meaningful actions they need to take to achieve better results. At the same time, they need to stay focused and not be distracted to hit their sales targets.

When under pressure, great salespeople need to be able to self-regulate so they are not paralyzed by fear or anxiety, and in turn, transfer those stresses onto internal colleagues. When facing demanding customers, great salespeople have the composure to handle demanding (and at times unreasonable) demands calmly and tactfully and then gain the support of internal colleagues to deal with those issues as a team.

Part 7

Motivating and Developing Your Sales Team

Winning the B2B Sale in China

Sometimes the first step towards motivating your sales team is to avoid demotivating them. As much as this seems to be common sense, my team and I have witnessed how a decision made by senior management demotivated the entire sales team.

That's right. Not an individual salesperson but demotivating the entire sales team. Here's what happened:

We had a client (a Training Manager) whose Sales Director wanted a 2-day business acumen training for their sales staff, in conjunction with their department's annual meeting.

After much discussion, we approved what the Sales Director wanted, and all was set for a rollout soon. Then, just 1 week before the workshop, the client called and said they had canceled it. Their Country Managing Director in China had vetoed it.

After further probing on our part, the Managing Director was initially undecided. It was their HR Director who vetoed, telling their Managing Director, "What's the purpose of up-skilling the salespeople in business acumen? It's better they don't know too much".

It turned out the HR Director had hired the Training Manager to conduct ALL workshops in-house to eliminate costs for external training. Also, being a former Legal Counsel, the HR Director was always mitigating the risks related to the sales department, in case the salespeople knew too much. They could act against the interests of the company. It might sound strange that a company would not trust its own sales team, but the legal profession has been trained to mitigate risks, no matter how remote they are.

While we might have lost some revenue in this episode, the more significant loss was for the client. This could be just the most efficient way to demotivate the entire sales team.

Firstly, the Sales Director lost face big time. He lost face with the cancellation of a workshop he had promised his team, and he would be losing more face during the annual meeting.

The Sales Director lost credibility too, for not being able to obtain benefits for his team. Hence the sales team might not be as willing to work harder for the Sales Director, much less the company. Vetoed by HR, no less.

Not surprisingly, the Sales Director soon left the company, followed by some key sales team members. On a bigger picture, though, such incidents also portrayed dysfunctional leadership at the helm.

Here's what happened in a company I used to work for in China. We had a sales manager who was in charge of the Taiwan market. She was promoted as Sales Manager because of her ability to sell, contributing to 60% of the entire region's sales revenue single-handedly. When she was promoted as Sales Manager, she was still focused on generating her personal sales revenue rather than developing her team to achieve more significant sales targets. So, while sales revenues for the Taiwan territory grew, it grew because the Taiwan Sales Manager's personal sales figures grew, at times at the expense of her team members. She would take away the better customers from her team members and make those her personal customers.

In addition, she also transgressed into the territories of other sales teams. As there were many Taiwanese companies (who were our target customers) that had expanded into Mainland China, these companies were deemed by management as customers belonging to Mainland China's sales territories. The Taiwan Sales Manager, however, tracked down these companies and got them as her customers.

When the salespeople in Mainland China found out about this transgression, they were agitated and distraught. Besides coping with very challenging sales targets, they now had part of their customer base being taken away by someone else. So, the Mainland China sales team complained to senior management, asking for the customers to be returned to them.

Instead of making a balanced or objective decision, however, management decided to do nothing. They feared upsetting the Taiwan Sales Manager much more than the salespeople in Mainland China. Their rationale was if they were to take action against the Taiwan Sales Manager, she might leave the company and take her customers to the competitor. Eventually, some of the Mainland China sales team's best performers left and worked for the competition!

According to Peter Drucker, work is accomplished by those employees who have not yet reached their level of incompetence, and people get promoted to their level of incompetence. Hence, it's not uncommon to have sales managers not knowing what they need to do. Some studies have shown that as low as 15% of superstar salespeople could be competent sales managers. The former role focuses on driving sales and handling customers, while the latter is a lot more about developing the sales team and coordinating with colleagues and partners to achieve team results. So, when a superstar salesperson is promoted to a sales manager, the company, in essence, has lost a great salesperson and hired an ineffective sales manager.

In greater detail, sales managers have to do the following:

Hiring. Many times sales managers are responsible for hiring the members of their teams. One key mistake sales managers tend to make is hiring people who are like them, unaware that they might require different selling styles for different customer segments. In general, a sales team needs to have a good balance of salespeople who can get new customers, or Hunters, and those who can keep and grow existing ones, known as Farmers. Getting Farmers to do Hunters' jobs is not likely to generate good results in the short term, and many sales managers do not have the patience to wait or develop them!

Some sales managers have adopted a strategy of hiring salespeople en masse. If the salesperson does not perform to expectations within 3-6 months, they would be fired. The process, it assumed, was the ones who could survive in such harsh conditions could become the next sales superstar. However, according to some studies, each salesperson who leaves prematurely could cost the company up to 2 years' worth of sales targets for the salesperson. Sales managers need to put more effort into ensuring the suitability of the candidates when hiring talents for their sales teams.

<u>Managing pipelines.</u> The key responsibility of any sales manager is to manage their team members' pipelines to ensure they meet their targets. Many sales managers, however, manage "numbers" rather than the pipelines. In their sales meetings, they asked salespeople for their numbers, or how much of their sales targets they have achieved, when reviewing their sales team's pipelines. Unfortunately, the sales figures quoted are simply the result of the salesperson's actions before getting the sales. What sales managers need to do would be to manage the end sales team's next step actions with each of their sales opportunities, instead of merely chasing "numbers".

A client in the IT industry was trying to shift from selling "boxes" aggressively to selling service subscriptions over a "lifecycle" period. They wanted to shift their emphasis from selling a considerable sum in one sales deal to actively engaging with the customer over multiple contact points and then selling subscriptions at those different contact points. As customers could cancel those subscriptions or opt-out to renew subscriptions, the salespeople would have to be less aggressive and spend more time and effort building trust with their customers.

However, being a publicly listed company, everyone from their CEO downwards was measured by quarterly results. Metrics such as "deal velocity" were constantly used to measure how fast those deals were happening. Hence instead of making the shift, the sales team struggled to meet the conflicting objectives of closing a sale as soon as possible and building long-term trust with the customer. As a way forward, that company was looking at better ways to manage their pipelines to balance both objectives..

Developing the team. When I asked the sales managers if they must train or coach their sales team, they all replied "yes". However, when I asked if they had a systematic way of training or coaching their sales team regularly, the answer was usually "no". The key reason was while up-skilling and developing the sales team is an important issue, it was seldom an "urgent" thing. In other words, if the sales manager postpones a training or coaching session, it's unlikely to cause immediate adverse effects. As sales managers tend to be very busy, such important but not urgent tasks tend to be postponed indefinitely, and their sales team remains under-developed.

The same IT client I mentioned above began to place a lot of emphasis on the coaching skills of their sales managers. Instead of merely telling salespeople what to do, their sales managers would then coach their team at appropriate times to improve their sales performance. While the sales managers might not have the luxury of upskilling their teams more systematically, they compensate through coaching their teams during their regular conversations.

<u>Resource allocation</u>. Sales managers are also in charge of allocating the right resources to meet their teams' sales targets. Some common resources sales managers may include allocating sales territories or leads for the respective salespeople, approving "special prices" or discounts for selected customers, and giving certain customers samples or extra spare parts.

Perhaps the most common of these resources would be to approve "special prices" or discounts when salespeople ask. However, in the words of one of our hospitality clients, "the free upgrade is usually given to customers who least deserve it". Many sales managers tend to approve such discounts just because the salesperson asked or simply to help the salesperson contribute to the sales target。 They often do not qualify which customers deserve such deals.

<u>Coordination</u>. One of the key unwritten job descriptions of any manager, sales or otherwise, would be to coordinate with other department's managers, such as the technical, customer service or supply chain departments, to fulfill customers' expectations. Customers' requirements could quickly outstrip the resources of other departments. Sales managers would then need to explore innovative ways to gain the support of other departments despite their busy schedules and the lack of sufficient resources.

If sales managers are not able to discharge the above duties well, they could become dysfunctional. The consequences would then be:

- Chronic low performance of the sales team, if not the company,
- Low engagement and high staff turnover of the best performing employees, and
- Creating a toxic work culture might require considerable efforts to undo even when the dysfunctional manager is long gone and may even prevent potential new talent from joining.

Hence, it becomes crucial for management to identify potentially dysfunctional sales managers in their respective organisations, and then find ways to reduce or correct the negative impacts of such dysfunctional behaviours.

Motivating the Sales Team

One common misconception about motivating

salespeople would be to pay them a good commission or bonus whenever they bring in the sale. Sales commissions and even sales competitions may not consistently deliver expected results when motivating salespeople. For instance, Apple Stores generate one of the highest sales per square foot of retail space in the retail industry. Yet, none of their retail employees are paid sales commissions.

In business-to-business sales, the effectiveness of purely using sales commissions as a sole motivating factor would be even lower. To understand how motivation works, here's a Motivation Equation to illustrate how people are motivated.

$$\text{MOTIVATION} = \frac{\text{Chances of Success} \times \text{Expected Payoff}}{\text{Amount of Effort}}$$

People will be motivated to do something IF they know they can succeed. The chances of success could be reliant on:

- Their skill level,
- The opportunities available, and
- The support and resources given.

It gets complicated when you look at the Expected Pay-off. In a way, it may seem to be monetary or material rewards, but there are many more pay-offs available, such as:

- Material rewards (salary increases, bonuses or other payments),
- Purpose (can I find meaning or a sense of purpose in my work),
- Recognition (public and private recognition of good contribution),
- Autonomy,
- Work-life balance, and
- Security (can I keep my job for the foreseeable future).

Many managers tend to focus on the top two and forget that middle managers could implement more cost-effective options other than money or career advancements.

But there is a different dimension to managing the expectation of Expected Pay-Offs, such as:

- How soon will the pay-off be?
- How frequent?
- How large or significant will it be?

In general, if the pay-off is not large enough, then people would want have it as quickly and as frequently as possible.

To illustrate this, we can use the case of industrial equipment or solution sales as an example. Typically, the sales cycle of industrial equipment can be months, if not years. So, if salespeople are looking forward to the monetary rewards of the sale, it will take a long while before they get anything.

The same goes for salespeople or even distributors who are tasked to sell new products. Some companies try to encourage their salespeople or distributors to sell new products by promising a higher sales commission or payout if those sales are made. Unfortunately, the results are usually mixed if not downright dismal. It would take a lot more time and effort to sell those new products, and the salespeople would rather make a quicker turnaround and thus sell more products by just focusing on selling existing products. If the sales manager also measures salespeople by their very short-term sales results, salespeople would be even more motivated to stick with selling current products, regardless how much more commission or bonus they could get if they sell new ones. They could even fear losing their jobs if they were selling new products but fall short of their sales targets.

So how can managers motivate salespeople dealing with long sales cycles and maintain their enthusiasm throughout the sales process? Here are some clues:

- Salespeople may feel motivated if they can advance the sale to the following stages. That can be a sense of achievement, or it can be a higher probability of eventual success.
- Salespeople may feel motivated along the way if they are getting support and resources from others in the company.
- Salespeople may be motivated if they are given frequent recognition for getting the right things done, such as gaining

appointments with the right people or putting up proposals that delight customers..

People will be inclined to do those things that require as little effort as possible to get what they want. Some of the factors that may reduce the amount of effort required are similar to those that increase chances of success, including:

- Training and coaching to improve skill level,
- Support, tools, and resources provided, and
- Teamwork.

Coaching Your Sales Team to Achieve Outstanding Results

Much of the feedback sales managers give their sales teams tends to sound like the following:

Sales Manager: So, what are your numbers currently?

Sales Person: Boss, it's xxx

Sales Manager: That's way behind your target! Go and go make some numbers!

Sales Person: Yes Boss!

And the same scenario keeps on playing over again and again. Unfortunately, doing so is not productive. Here are the reasons why:

By focusing on the "numbers", neither the sales manager nor the salesperson knows what is preventing them from achieving better results. A conversation needs to be conducted to discover the actions taken and what actions need to be taken next.

Of course, there will be sales managers who give the salesperson exact orders such as:

- "Go make more calls!"
- "Go chase after the customer!"
- "Go push the (higher priced) product!"

While these could be the right actions to take depending on the situation, the reality is only the salesperson has first-hand information on what's going on and might have a clearer perspective on what needs to be done. Who knows if the salesperson has already done what the sales manager asked, but to no avail, and would need help and support to devise better sales strategies? There could be deeper underlying reasons that require further probing and discovery to uncover the path to outstanding performance.

Just as the adage "Selling ain't Telling" implies, developing a salesperson's abilities is not simply telling the salesperson what to do. In many instances, the salesperson might have some ideas about how to do their job. They might also be making some headway in their work. However, the results they get may not be coming fast enough to meet sales targets.

So as managers, the coaching will be to find out:

- What is the situation, as well as the contextual causes of that situation?
- What is the goal or outcome the salesperson wants to achieve?
- What have they been doing so far?
- What kinds of support do they need to take the next step?

To illustrate further, here's a typical case many sales managers have encountered:

Jack is a new salesperson who works hard. He visits many customers consistently every day. Yet, despite all the hard work, he is unable to close many sales. Of the deals he has closed, most are small amounts at low prices. As such, he does not meet his targets.

A typical sales manager would have told Jack:

- You need to target better customers,
- You need to sell bigger or higher value, and
- You need to withstand price pressures.

Now, this is sensible advice for the salesperson. However, that does not take into consideration whether Jack:

- Has tried out those ideas, but they did not seem to work,
- Has hit some obstacles and did not know how to overcome them, or
- Is at a loss what could be a practical next step..

This is when the sales manager needs to use a

different approach, such as coaching.

The Sales Manager can approach Jack and start by framing the Topic and gaining agreement:

"I see you are behind in your sales targets. Is there something we can discuss to see how to improve those numbers?"

In most circumstances, Jack is going to say yes and agree. The Sales Manager can then ask for an Outcome that is achievable and will lead to concrete actions:

"So, what would be an Outcome you would like to achieve today?"

Jack could address a specific area where he would like to get help or express something he would like to improve. These areas could be:

- How to gain appointments with the right people,
- How to know if the customer is worth pursuing, or
- How to overcome initial objections such as "no need" or "too expensive".

Whatever the case, it's important that the Sales Manager NOT give any advice yet. Instead, the Sales Manager could Explore Possibilities by asking powerful questions such as:

- "So, what have you done so far?"
- "What do you think will make the customer

want to see you?"
- "What do you think the customer means when they say that?"
- "What else could be a different response to that?"
- "How would you gauge the level of their interest?"

The key thing is to make the salesperson reflect and clarify what has been done (or not done). As the adage goes, "teach a man to fish, and you feed him for a lifetime". If the salesperson could gain some insights on what could be done better, that salesperson would have improved his sales skills..

While exploring possibilities, it is also essential for the Sales Manager to:

- Show empathy and validate whatever strengths the salesperson has demonstrated or things he has done right, such as "I see you have been following your leads rigorously."
- Share your observations of the salesperson, including their feelings and emotions, for example. "I sense you are feeling frustrated with the customer's responses. Do you feel frustrated at times?"
- Create awareness by asking the salesperson what insights he has gained or learned from the conversation.

Based on the insights gained above, the Sales Manager can then work together with the salesperson to map out what actions to take. It would be even better if the Sales Manager could ask, "so what will be some follow-up actions you need to take?" When the salesperson provides the action steps, they are more likely to be accountable for the results.

Actions can be a wide variety of things, as long as it helps the salesperson achieve his outcome:

- "I need to reorganize the way I approach customers",
- "I need training in conducting price negotiations", or
- "I need to bring our engineer to see the customer".

Some actions might need a due date, while others can assume that the salesperson will adjust his behaviours in the next sales situation. In any case, the Sales Manager will hold the salesperson accountable in future meetings or coaching sessions.

Finally, the Sales Manager could ask for some Feedback from the salesperson about how the session has been helpful, and if there might be any ways to make future sessions more effective.

Some traditional sales managers might feel coaching might be a too "soft" to get results from salespeople. That couldn't be further from the truth. Although coaching allows the salesperson a lot of space to express themselves, eventually, the salesperson will still have to be accountable for results.

For the Sales Manager, not all conversations with their direct reports would be coaching conversations. Many times, Sales Managers have to give direct feedback or instructions. Through coaching the salesperson, there are times that sales managers could enable the sales team to make better judgments and decisions throughout the sales process. In other words, by allowing the salesperson to reflect on their situation and explore his options and actions, coaching can be a more effective way to get your sales team to achieve outstanding results!

Epilogue

While the stories shared in this book took place in China, similar stories probably could be found in many parts of the world too. As such, the sales strategies and tactics shared could also be used universally. Some of us might have heard about similar stories before or might have even encountered similar situations.

In any case, many effective sales strategies are counter-intuitive yet straightforward at times. The key thing is: what actions are you going to take to help you deal with similar situations in the future, whatever and wherever they could be?

I look forward to hearing your stories too, and we could also connect on social media. Please visit my LinkedIn account:

https://www.linkedin.com/in/cydj001/ and share your stories!

In the meantime, I have co-authored Sales Map, a sales proficiency assessment that gauges your strengths and weaknesses of every step throughout your sales process. With the Sales Map, you and your sales team can take the guesswork out of pinpointing which areas need to be strengthened so that you achieve better sales performance.

Since you have gotten this far from this book, I'd like to give you a free account for the assessment. Send a message to me on LinkedIn stating

"Winning the B2B Sale with Sales Map",

and I'll send you information on how to get your gift.

I look forward to hearing from you soon!

www.ingramcontent.com/pod-product-compliance
Lightning Source LLC
Chambersburg PA
CBHW071521220526
45472CB00003B/1107